LS7AE 09182

(Wed

15-

Academic Graffiti

My First Name, *Wystan*,
Rhymes with *Tristan*,
But—O dear!—I do hope
I'm not quite such a dope.

Academic Graffiti

W. H. AUDEN

Illustrated by Filippo Sanjust

FABER AND FABER LIMITED
3 Queen Square, London

First published in 1971
by Faber and Faber Limited
3 Queen Square, London W.C.1.
Printed in Great Britain by
Latimer Trend & Co. Ltd. Whitstable

ISBN 0 571 09380 9

In Memoriam
Ogden Nash

Forenote

About half of these clerihews were printed in my
volume *Homage to Clio*. I reprint them without shame
because I know that my verses are a small matter,
compared to Filippo Sanjust's illustrations.

W. H. A.

1
Henry Adams
Was mortally afraid of Madams:
In a disorderly house
He sat quiet as a mouse.

2

St. Thomas Aquinas
Always regarded wine as
A medicinal juice
That helped him to deduce.

3

Johann Sebastian Bach
Was a master of his *Fach*:
Nothing could be more *kluge*
Than his Kunst der Fuge.

4

Thomas Lovell Beddoes
Could never walk through meadows
Without getting the glooms
And thinking of tombs.

5

Ludwig van Beethoven
Believed it proven
That, for mortal dust,
What must be, must.

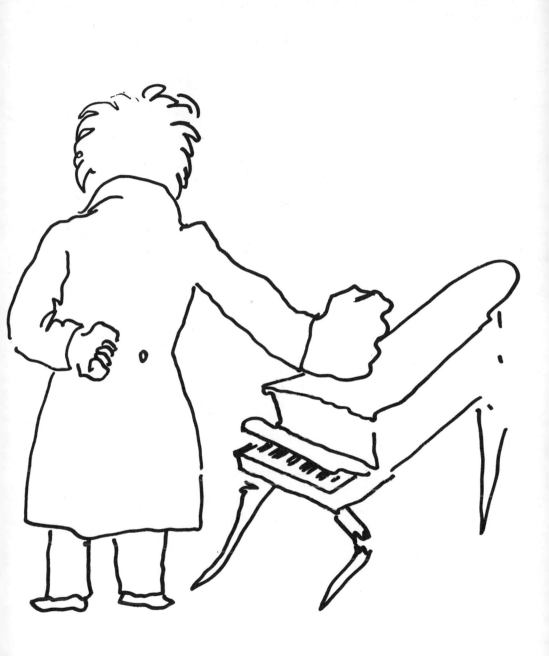

6
Good Queen Bess
Couldn't have liked it less,
When Burghley and Cecil
Drank out of the same vessel.

7

William Blake
Found Newton hard to take,
And was not enormously taken
With Francis Bacon.

8
Said Robert Bridges,
When badly bitten by midges:
'They're only doing their duty
As a testament to my beauty.'

9

Robert Browning
Immediately stopped frowning
And started to blush,
When fawned on by Flush.

10

Martin Buber
Never said 'Thou' to a tuber:
Despite his creed,
He did not feel the need.

11

Lord Byron

Once succumbed to a Siren:

His flesh was weak,

Hers Greek.

12

Among the prosodists, Bysshe[1]
Was the syllable-counting old sissy,
Guest[2].
The accentual pest.

[1]Edward Bysshe. Author of *Art of Poetry* (1702)
[2]Edwin Guest. Author of *History of English Rhythms*
(2 vols; 1836–38)

13
When Arthur Hugh Clough
Was jilted by a piece of fluff,
He sighed 'Quel dommage!',
And wrote *Amours de Voyages*.

14
Dante
Was utterly *enchanté*,
When Beatrice cried in tones that were
    peachy:
Noi siamo amici.

15
Hugo De Vries
During a visit to Greece
Composed a pastoral poem,
Xylem & Phloem.

16
Charles Dickens
Could find nothing to say to chickens,
But gossipping with rabbits
Became one of his habits.

17
Desiderius Erasmus
Always avoided chiasmus,
But grew addicted as time wore on
To oxymoron.

18
Fulke Greville
Wrote beautifully at sea level:
With each rising contour his verse
Got progressively worse.

19
The *Geheimrat* in Goethe
Made him all the curter
With *Leute* who were leery
Of his Colour Theory.

20
Sir Rider Haggard,
Was completely staggered
When his bride-to-be
Announced 'I AM SHE!'

21
Georg Friedrich Händel
Was highly respected in Kendal:
It was George Frederick Handel
Who caused all the scandal.

22
Thomas Hardy
Was never tardy
When summoned to fulfill
The Immanent Will.

23

Joseph Haydn
Never read Dryden
Nor did John Dryden
Ever hear Haydn.

24

No one could ever inveigle
Georg Wilhelm Friedrich Hegal
Into offering the slightest apology
For his *Phenomenology*.

25

George Herbert[1]
Once tried ordering sherbet
On Salisbury plain:
He ordered in vain.

[1] 17th-century religious poet; Rector of Bemerton, near Salisbury

26
Robert Herrick[1]
Certainly did not write *Eric*:
So far
As we know, it was Dean Farrar.

[1] Herrick was a 17th-century poet and gallant. *Eric, or Little by Little* by Dean Farrer was a famous Victorian school story

Robert Herrick

27
Henry James
Abhorred the word *Dames*,
And always wrote '*Mommas*'
With inverted commas.

28

When the young Kant
Was told to kiss his aunt,
He obeyed the Categorical Must,
But only just.

29
Søren Kierkegaard
Tried awfully hard
To take The Leap
But fell in a heap.

30
Karl Kraus[1]
Always had some grouse
Among his bête noires
Were Viennese choirs.

[1] Austrian satirist, d. 1936

31
Archbishop Laud
Was High, not Broad:
He could never descend
To celebrating at the North End.

32
Edward Lear
Was haunted by a fear
While travelling in Albania
Of contracting kleptomania.

33
Joseph Lister,
According to his sister,
Was not an alcoholic:
His vice was carbolic.

34

Mr. Robert Liston[1]
Used the saw like a piston:
He was *that* elated,
When he amputated.

[1] Robert Liston, (1794–1847). Surgeon in Edinburgh. It was said that he could take off a leg at the thigh in twenty-six seconds. He was also the first surgeon in Great Britain to perform an operation under anaesthesia

35

Luther & Zwingli
Should be treated singly:
L hated the Peasants,
Z the Real Presence.

36
Mallarmé
Had too much to say:
He could never quite
Leave the paper white.

37
Mary, Queen of Scots,
Could tie the most complicated knots,
But she couldn't bake
The simplest cake.

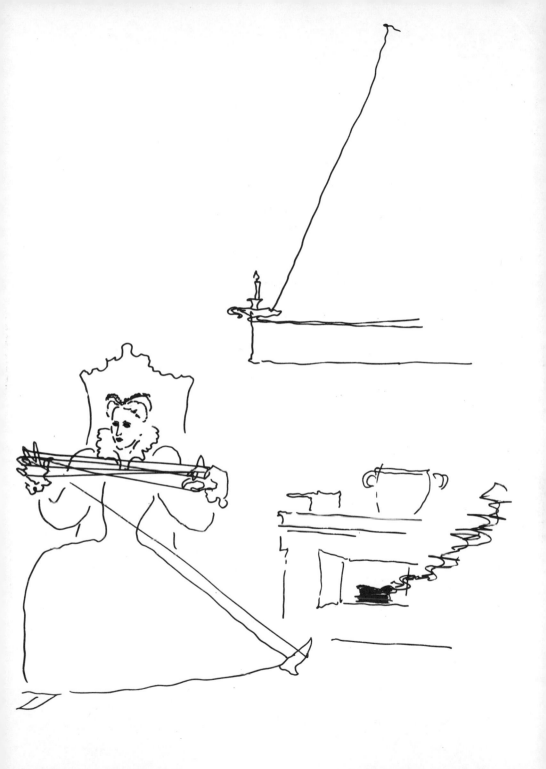

38
Queen Mary (The Bloody)
Had an understudy
Who was a Prot:
She was not.

39

When Karl Marx
Found the phrase 'financial sharks',
He sang a Te Deum
In the British Museum.

40
John Milton
Never stayed in a Hilton
Hotel,
Which was just as well.

41
William Henry Monk[1]
Lived in a perpetual blue funk
Of being taken on hikes
By John Bacchus Dykes[2].

[1] W. H. Monk (1823–89) composer of famous hymn-tunes,
e.g. for *Abide with me*
[2] J. B. Dykes (1823–76) composer of famous hymn-tunes,
e.g. for *Holy, holy, holy*

42
Thomas Moore
Caused a furore
Every time he bellowed his
Irish Melodies.

43
Cardinal Newman
Was being only human
When he dreamed of panning
The latest tract by Cardinal Manning.

44
Nietzsche
Had the habit as a teacher
Of cracking his joints
To emphasise his points.

45

Oxbridge philosophers, to be cursory,
Are products of a middle-class nursery:
Their arguments are anent
What Nanny really meant.

46
Louis Pasteur,
So his colleagues aver,
Lived on excellent terms
With most of his germs.

47

Alexander Pope
Never gave up hope
Of finding a motto
To affix to his Grotto.

48
Christina Rosetti
Thought it rather petty,
When her brother, D.G.,
Put laudanum in her tea.

49
When Sir Walter Scott
Made a blot,
He stamped with rage
And started a new page.

50

'*Ma foi!*', exclaimed Stendal,
'*Ce Scarpia n'est pas si mal,*
But he's no Count Mosca,
Unluckily for Tosca.'

51
Adalbert Stifter[1]
Was no weight-lifter
He would hire old lags
To carry his bags.

[1] Austrian writer of the Biedermayer period

52
William Makepeace Thackery
Wept into his daiquiri,
When he heard St. John's Wood
Thought he was no good.

53
Thomas the Rhymer
Was probably a social climber:
He should have known Fairy Queens
Were beyond his means.

54
Thomas Traherne[1]
Could always discern
The Angel in boys,
Even when they made a noise.

[1] 17th-century mystical poet, forerunner
of Wordsworth

55
Paul Valéry
Earned a meagre salary,
Walking through the *Bois*,
Observing his *Moi*.

56
Good Queen Victoria
In a fit of euphoria
Commanded Disraeli
To blow up the Old Bailey.

57
James Watt
Was the hard-boiled kind of Scot:
He thought any dream
Sheer waste of steam.

58
Oscar Wilde
Was greatly beguiled,
When into the Cafe Royal walked Bosie
Wearing a tea-cosy.

59
Sir Thomas Wyatt
Never went on a diet,
Unlike the Earl of Surrey,
Who ate nothing but curry.

60

Whenever Xantippe
Wasn't feeling too chippy,
She would bawl at Socrates:
'Why aren't you Hippocrates?'